by Zachary Cohn

illustrated by Susan Frankenberry

Scott Foresman
is an imprint of

Glenview, Illinois • Boston, Massachusetts • Mesa, Arizona
Shoreview, Minnesota • Upper Saddle River, New Jersey

Every effort has been made to secure permission and provide appropriate credit for photographic material. The publisher deeply regrets any omission and pledges to correct errors called to its attention in subsequent editions.

Unless otherwise acknowledged, all photographs are the property of Pearson.

Photo locations denoted as follows: Top (T), Center (C), Bottom (B), Left (L), Right (R), Background (Bkgd)

Illustrations by Susan Frankenberry

Photograph 8 Digital Vision

ISBN 13: 978-0-328-39294-0
ISBN 10:   0-328-39294-4

You saw the bird
in your tree.

You saw the bird
at your vet.

You saw the cat
on your grass.

You saw the cat
at your vet.

The vet helps
small animals.

Animal Shelters

Like many living things, animals need shelter, food, water, and air. Animal shelters are places that can help meet these needs. Some of these places have vets who can help heal sick or injured animals.

Helping animals is a great thing to do. But if you find an animal that is lost or hurt, you should not touch it. It may not be safe. Ask an adult you know for help. Call an animal shelter, and they can help the animal get better!